For those brave enough to try.

How to Become an Influencer: Your Ultimate Guide to Becoming an Influencer by: Savannah Jane

First Printing, 2024
Published: 2024, Amazon

Cover Design by Savannah Jane

Sources: Forbes, Grazitti, Winsavvy, Kubbco, Novatomato, Press.farm, Cipio, Medium, Territory Influence - LinkedIn, Moburst, Faster Capital, Valeriainc , Medium, AIcontentfy, Digital Delane, IntechOpen, Socioblend, Social Media Today, Hootsuite, Buffer, Sprout Social, Investopedia, Rock House Financial, Mesha Club, WIS Accountancy, Afluencer, HubSpot, Buffer, CoSchedule, StoryBrand, AdEspresso, Canva Pro, Amazon, Jasper AI

Here we go...

CHAPTER 1: UNDERSTANDING THE WORLD OF INFLUENCER MARKETING

In today's digital age, the world of influencer marketing has become a powerful and lucrative industry. From Instagram to YouTube, influencers have the ability to captivate audiences and shape trends. In this chapter, we'll explore the concept of influencer marketing, the impact it has on consumer behavior, and why becoming an influencer can be an exciting and rewarding career path.

Navigating the complex landscape of social media, you may wonder how you can turn your passion and creativity into a successful influencer career. This chapter will provide you with a foundation for understanding the dynamics of influencer marketing and the opportunities it presents for individuals like yourself.

Types of Influencers:
- Mega-Influencers: 1 million or more followers
- Macro-Influencers: 100,000 – 1 million followers
- Mid-Tier Influencers: 20,000 – 100,000 followers
- Micro-Influencers: 1,000 – 100,000 followers
- Nano-Influencers: 1,000 – 10,000 followers

These categories are often differentiated based on their follower count, reach, and level of influence within specific niches or industries. Understanding the distinctions between these influencer types can be valuable for brands and marketers when devising influencer marketing strategies or collaborations.

Types of Influencer Niches & Industries:
Food Influencers, Health and Wellness Influencers, Fashion Influencers, Lifestyle Influencers, Sports and Fitness Influencers, Gamers, Bloggers/Vloggers, Photographers, Travel and Tourism Influencers, Beauty Influencers. The list could go on – you probably know an influencer for every category here. It's like a who's who of the internet's cool cats! These categories encompass a wide range of influencer types, each catering to specific interests and industries.

Being an influencer, is to be an entrepreneur. So buckle up.

CHAPTER 2: UNDERSTANDING YOUR NICHE

Before diving headfirst into the world of influencer marketing, it's crucial to understand the importance of personal branding. Your personal brand is a reflection of who you are, what you stand for, and the value you bring to your audience. This chapter will guide you through the process of discovering and defining your unique personal brand, helping you stand out in the crowded social media landscape.

We will discuss the significance of authenticity, consistency, and storytelling in building a compelling personal brand. Additionally, we'll provide actionable tips and exercises to help you unearth your passions, strengths, and the message you want to convey to your audience.

What Does It Mean?

Finding your niche in the market entails pinpointing a specific area of expertise, interest, or demographic that sets you apart from others in your industry. Your niche defines the unique value you bring to the table and serves as the foundation for building your personal brand. It is about identifying the intersection of your passions, skills, and the needs of your target audience.

Navigating the Challenges

One of the primary difficulties in finding your niche is the fear of narrowing your focus too much, potentially alienating a broader audience.

Capitalizing on Your Niche:

Discover Your Passion – 1
To begin the journey of finding your niche, introspection is crucial. Reflect on your passions, interests, and the topics that ignite your enthusiasm. Look for areas where your expertise and genuine interest intersect, as this forms the foundation of a compelling personal brand.

Research Your Audience – 2
Understanding your target audience is pivotal in identifying a niche that resonates with them. Conduct thorough research to comprehend the needs, pain points, and preferences of your audience within your industry. This insight will guide you towards tailoring your niche to align with the demands of your potential followers.

Authenticity is Key – 3
While it may be tempting to emulate successful brands, authenticity is paramount in carving out your niche. Your personal brand should reflect your unique personality, values, and voice. Embrace what sets you apart, as this authenticity will attract an engaged and loyal audience.

Consistency and Adaptability – 4
Consistency in delivering content within your niche establishes credibility and fosters trust with your audience. Balancing consistency with adaptability ensures that your brand remains relevant and resilient.

Engage and Listen – 5
Engaging with your audience and actively listening to their feedback is a powerful tool in refining your niche. Pay attention to the content that generates the most engagement and address the pain points expressed by your audience. This iterative process will help you fine-tune your niche over time.

What makes you different from the rest?
THAT is your niche.

CHAPTER 3: BUILDING A STRONG PERSONAL BRAND

Your personal brand is your superhero cape as an influencer! Unveil the secrets to crafting a powerful personal brand that screams YOU - values, quirks, and all. From finding your special brand voice to nailing a snazzy visual style, we're here to lead you on a quest to build a memorable and impactful personal brand. Mastering the art of branding will make you shine like a diamond in the heap of online noise, attracting the coolest collabs and partnerships your way.

By defining your brand voice, you'll chat with your audience like an old pal on every platform. Your logo, colors, and overall look should be a symphony of awesomeness, making your brand unforgettable.

1. Get your profiles in order. Don't look like a fool.
2. Lame I know, but be yourself.
3. Share your "slogan/niche".
4. Join industry groups on social media and follow people that relate to your niche.
5. Engage with people online, build connections and inspire others.
6. Don't just focus on one social media platform, connect with people on other platforms and then redirect them to the platform you want to focus on.
7. Make sure your profile is in "business/professional" setting to gather analytics.
8. Create an aesthetic that works for you, and make sure to stay consistent with your "style".
9. Post all kinds of content. Seriously though, images, videos, polls, do it all.
10. To make life easier use cross-platform tools. Such as Hootsuite or Sprout Social
11. Lastly, stay consistent. Make a schedule to post and stick to it.

Tip: Learn the lingo the youths are using. Trust me you'll have more Ws than Ls.

CHAPTER 4: ENGAGING WITH YOUR AUDIENCE

Successful influencers understand the significance of meaningful engagement with their audience. This chapter will focus on cultivating genuine connections with your followers, fostering a sense of community, and leveraging various social media platforms to interact with your audience.

In today's digital age, being an influencer goes beyond just having a large following. It's about building relationships and creating valuable interactions with your audience. Authenticity is key when it comes to connecting with your followers. Showcasing your personality, sharing your story, and being relatable can help form genuine connections that resonate with your audience.

Creating a sense of community among your followers can further strengthen these connections. Encouraging discussions, hosting Q&A sessions, or even organising meet-ups can foster a feeling of belonging and unity within your follower base. This sense of community not only keeps your audience engaged but also encourages them to become active participants in your journey.

Utilising various social media platforms is essential in reaching a wider audience and engaging with different demographics. Each platform offers unique features and caters to different types of content, so understanding how to optimise your presence on each platform can help you connect with a diverse range of followers.

Active listening and responding to feedback are crucial aspects of engagement. Your followers want to feel heard and valued, so taking the time to acknowledge their comments, answer their questions, and address their concerns can go a long way in building trust and loyalty. This two-way communication shows that you care about your audience's opinions and are committed to providing them with valuable content.

By mastering the art of engagement, you have the opportunity to cultivate a dedicated fan base that not only supports your work but also becomes a part of your influencer journey. Remember, it's not just about the numbers; it's about the meaningful connections you create with your audience that truly make you a successful influencer.

Interacting with your followers doesn't guarantee they're saints. Some are straight up terrible human beings.

CHAPTER 5: MONETIZING YOUR INFLUENCE

Monetizing your influence is the ultimate goal for many aspiring influencers. In this final chapter, we'll explore diverse revenue streams available to influencers, such as brand partnerships, sponsored content, affiliate marketing, and digital product creation. We'll also discuss the significance of negotiation skills, understanding your worth, and maintaining authenticity while collaborating with brands. By strategically monetizing your influence, you can turn your passion into a sustainable and lucrative career, empowering you to thrive as a successful entrepreneur in the digital age.

What are brand partnerships:

Brand partnerships refer to collaborations between two or more brands to leverage each other's strengths and reach a wider audience. These partnerships can come in various forms, such as co-branded products, joint marketing campaigns, or sponsored events. By joining forces, brands can tap into each other's customer base, increase brand visibility, and create unique experiences that resonate with consumers.

What is sponsored content:

Sponsored content on social media refers to posts or articles that are paid for by an advertiser to promote a specific product, service, or brand. These posts are usually clearly marked as "sponsored" or "paid partnership" to distinguish them from regular organic content. Sponsored content can come in various formats, such as sponsored posts, stories, videos, or influencer collaborations.

What is affiliate marketing:

Affiliate marketing on social media involves partnering with influencers, content creators, or other users who promote products or services on their platforms in exchange for a commission on sales generated through their unique affiliate links. This strategy leverages the influencer's reach and credibility to drive traffic and sales for the merchant.

NEGOTIATION TIPS AND TRICKS.

Calling all social media stars! Wanna rake in the cash? Well, buckle up as we dive into the world of negotiation skills for influencers. Picture this: influencers flaunting their worth, dazzling brands with their stats, and sealing the deal with finesse.

Step one: Know thyself! Influencers, show off your strengths and data to prove your value. It's all about snagging that sweet deal that matches your brand power.

Step two: Sharpen those communication skills! Speak up, be clear, and watch those partnerships bloom. It's all about finding that win-win scenario with brands.

Next up: Flexibility is key! Be willing to bend a little, find that sweet spot where both you and the brand hit the jackpot. It's a dance of compromise and creativity.

Oh, and don't forget to network like a pro! Rub shoulders with fellow influencers and industry bigwigs to boost your negotiating game. Power in numbers, right?

When an influencer engages in negotiations with a brand, it is essential to approach the conversation with professionalism and clear communication. Here is an example of how the negotiation conversation might unfold:

Influencer: Hello [Brand Representative], thank you for considering a potential collaboration with me. I believe that our partnership could be mutually beneficial and create valuable content for both our audiences.

Brand Representative: Hello [Influencer], we are excited about the possibility of working with you. Could you please share more about your ideas for the collaboration and your rates?

Influencer: Of course! I have a few concepts in mind that I believe would resonate well with my followers and align with your brand values. In terms of rates, I typically charge [insert rates or negotiation terms] for similar collaborations. I am open to discussing this further and finding a solution that works for both of us.

Brand Representative: Thank you for sharing your ideas and rates. We appreciate your transparency and professionalism. Let's discuss how we can move forward with this collaboration and ensure that it is a win-win for both parties.

Influencer: That sounds great. I am looking forward to working together and creating engaging content that showcases your brand in an authentic way. I am open to further discussions and finding common ground to make this collaboration a success.

Remember, open communication, understanding each other's needs, and being willing to negotiate are key elements in a successful influencer-brand collaboration.

Confidence. Even if it's fake.

UNDERSTANDING YOUR WORTH.

Knowing your value is key in the realm of influencing!

By researching other influencers and their **media kits**, you can gain valuable insights into the industry standards for partnerships and brand collaborations. This knowledge will not only help you negotiate fair compensation for your work but also showcase your professionalism to potential partners. Remember, your worth is not just about the numbers but also about the value you bring to the table with your unique voice and perspective.

Keep learning, growing, and advocating for yourself in your influencer journey.

What is an influencer media kit?

An influencer media kit is a valuable tool that content creators use to showcase their work, highlight their strengths, and provide important information to potential collaborators and brands. It typically includes a brief introduction about the influencer, their niche or area of expertise, audience demographics, past collaborations, rates, services offered, and contact information. A well-designed influencer media kit can help influencers stand out in a competitive market and attract partnerships that align with their brand and values. It serves as a professional portfolio that demonstrates the influencer's reach, engagement, and the value they can bring to a brand's marketing campaigns.

Okay. Let's get into the fun stuff.

NEED MORE INFORMATION?
LETS GO TO THE INTERNET.

Now, listen up! This book might play hard to get, but hey, it's just a friendly nudge in the right direction. Packed with info nuggets to light your path, but hey, let's face it - diving into the online search sea can feel like a wild goose chase! Fear not, below are some secret search tips to help you on your influencer journey!

How to become a successful influencer? 🔍

Who are the top 10 influencers in [country]? 🔍

How to make money as an Influencer? 🔍

Best social media platform to make money. 🔍

What are the newest types of influencers? 🔍

Tthe best Influencer marketing tools 2024 🔍

Sprout Social's blog

Secure you profile for Influencer's Safety

When to post of social media 2024

Different AI tools that influencers can use

Trending audio for reels/tiktoks

List of different types of content

Trending hashtags/topics

[Influencer] media kit

Best SEO for Influencer marketing?

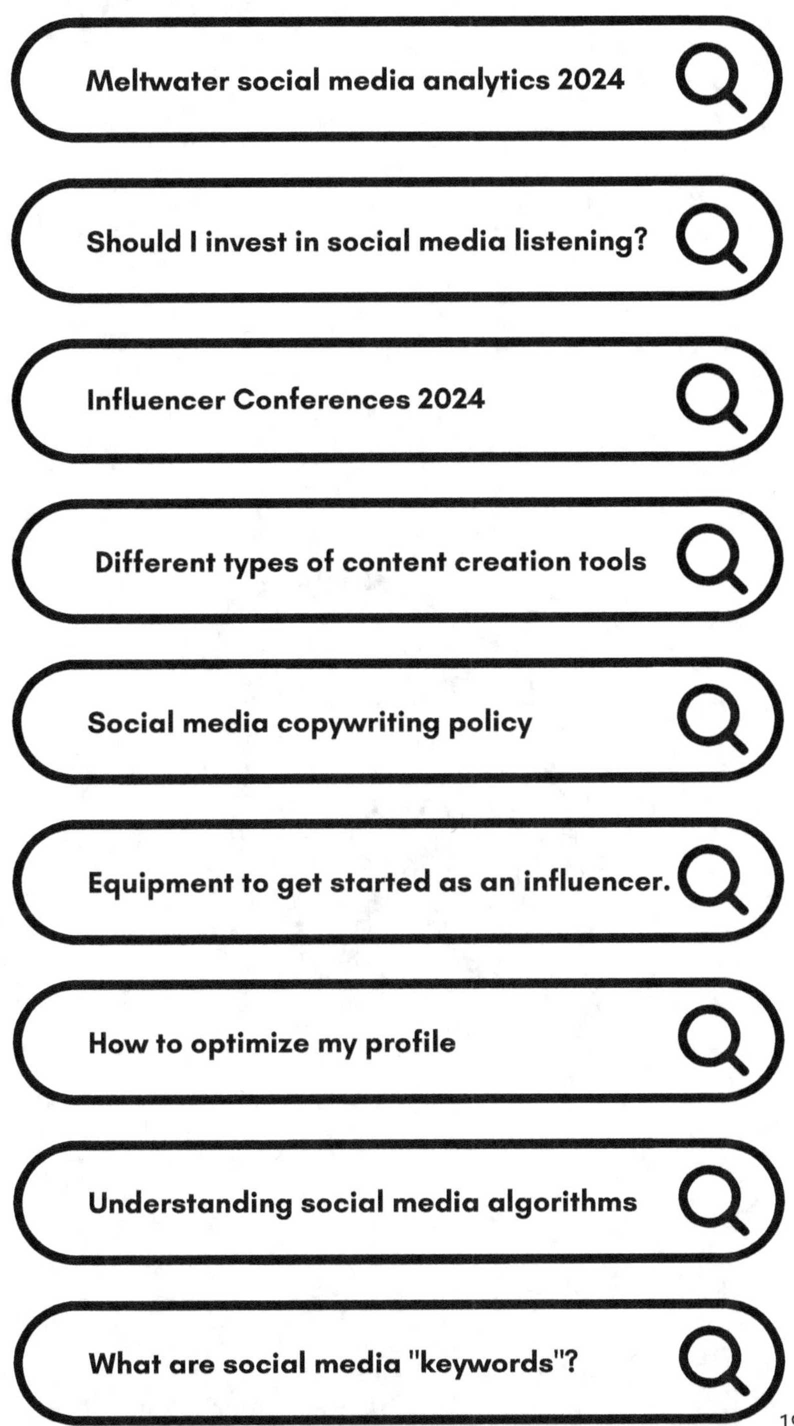

Meltwater social media analytics 2024
Should I invest in social media listening?
Influencer Conferences 2024
Different types of content creation tools
Social media copywriting policy
Equipment to get started as an influencer.
How to optimize my profile
Understanding social media algorithms
What are social media "keywords"?

Hope this helped.

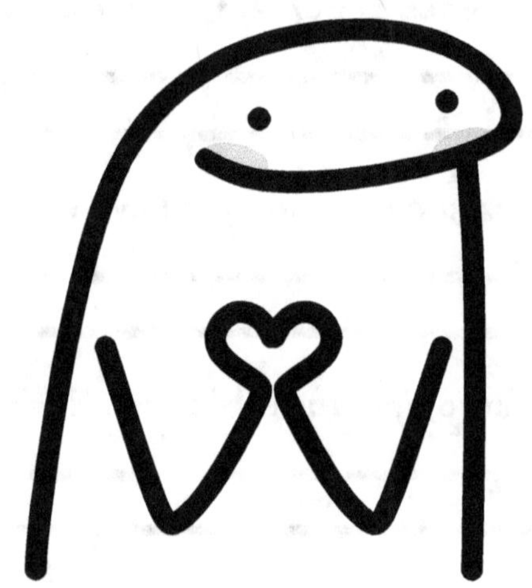

How to Become an Influencer: Your Ultimate Guide to Becoming an Influencer by: Savannah Jane

First Printing, 2024
Published: 2024, Amazon

Cover Design by Savannah Jane

Sources: Forbes, Grazitti, Winsavvy, Kubbco, Novatomato, Press.farm, Cipio, Medium, Territory Influence - LinkedIn, Moburst, Faster Capital, Valeriainc , Medium, AIcontentfy, Digital Delane, IntechOpen, Socioblend, Social Media Today, Hootsuite, Buffer, Sprout Social, Investopedia, Rock House Financial, Mesha Club, WIS Accountancy, Afluencer, HubSpot, Buffer, CoSchedule, StoryBrand, AdEspresso, Canva Pro, Amazon, Jasper AI